[redacted]

ANCIENT MUSIC

Also by Stephen Edgar
QUEUING FOR THE MUDD CLUB

ANCIENT MUSIC

Stephen Edgar

ANGUS & ROBERTSON PUBLISHERS

Angus & Robertson Publishers' creative writing programme is assisted by the Australia Council, the Federal Government's arts funding and advisory body.

ANGUS & ROBERTSON PUBLISHERS

Unit 4, Eden Park, 31 Waterloo Road, North Ryde, NSW, Australia 2113, and 16 Golden Square, London W1R 4BN, United Kingdom

*First published in Australia by Angus & Robertson Publishers in 1988
First published in the United Kingdom by Angus & Robertson (UK) in 1988*

*National Library of Australia
Cataloguing-in-publication data.*

*Edgar, Stephen, 1951– .
Ancient music.
ISBN 0 207 15698 0.
I. Title.
A821'.3*

*Typeset in 10 pt English Times
Printed in Singapore*

Acknowledgements

Some of these poems have appeared in the *Adelaide Review, Age, Australian Literary Magazine, Island Magazine, Mercury, Quadrant, Westerly* and the anthologies *An Inflection of Silence* (University of Newcastle, 1986) and *Poems Selected from the Australian's 20th Anniversary Competition* (Angus & Robertson, 1985).

The poem "Dr Rogers' Report" is based on a letter received by a friend of mine from an English friend of hers, one Dr Brian Rogers, who had recently returned from a photographic expedition through Central and South America. His letter contained such a vivid account of this trip that, on being permitted to read it, I was moved to turn it into a poem, in Spenserian stanzas as it happened. Apart from abridgement and the liberties necessary to transform prose into verse the poem is, or was intended to be, faithful to the letter, both in the events described and the language that describes them.

"Li Tsung-ping" is based on a scene in the film *Dersu Uzala* by Akira Kurosawa.

"Rapunzel": it is probably unnecessary to point out that rapunzel is simply the German word for rampion, the plant which Rapunzel's mother had a craving for and sent her husband to fetch from the witch's garden. Not all English versions of the tale make this irony of naming clear.

I would like to thank the Literature Board of the Australia Council for a New Writer's Fellowship during 1986 which enabled me to write many of the poems in this book.

Contents

78s

Even when I was young they were worn out,
Lying like heirlooms that have lost their use
But must be kept.
They were so present, so full of weight,
A solidness that would impress
A child. But those old needles scraped
The music off too soon. Their life was short.

I'd take an album out from time to time,
Its binding faded in maroon or blue,
And turn the heavy
Sleeves, watching in their circles the tame
Dogs fall, the falling dust a cue
For silence. Only one I ever
Heard, *The Thieving Magpie,* its sudden drum-

Roll giving notice of another music,
Peremptory under its ruined sound.
My father never
Played them. Having shut away his stock
Before the war he'd come to find
That their performance was now over.
And if I felt he'd sleeved away there disc

By disc something they harboured of himself
The two of us could put on obsolescence
As well as they
Could. All secrets were quite safe
In our technology of silence.
He couldn't speak to me, nor I
To him. We worked for years to perfect that gulf.

The new equipment goes without their speed.
Lying in dust they still have to be saved,
Memorable
Not in themselves, though still as hard

And weighty, since really they're preserved
In negatives, unplayable,
Unheard, like everything that wasn't said.

Two Crows

An Adaptation of Twa Corbies

As I was walking all alone
I heard two crows' sardonic moan,
And over me their cawing fell
Like a displacing trance or spell,

Until through monochrome vision I'm
Abstracted to a changeless time.
Their caws are speech. I hear one say,
"Where shall we go and dine today?"

"Below us on the grass-grey plain
I see a faceless soldier slain.
What might be colour on his cheek
Is but the smear his gashes leak.

"How many hours did it take
Of dying dreams that soon he'd wake
Elsewhere, till slow degrees of cold
Whited out the lies they told?

"His comrades like ice in the sun,
As though they never were, have gone,
And not a soul knows where he lies
Who is overlooked here by the skies.

"In distant houses coped with cloud
Grey figures watch an empty shroud
But will, before too long, replace
The forgotten voice, the faded face.

"His lady, wasted now from love,
Once more will couple soon enough,
But briefly shamed to find it sweet.
So let us too set down to eat.

"You'll unstring his shattered thigh
And I'll peck out a shocked grey eye.
With every strand of his sun-white hair
We'll thatch our nest when it grows bare.

"None shall find him, but their moans
Hang in the wind that will parch his bones
Forever (listen!) when they're bare."
I woke. The wind was in my hair.

Understudies

Did Golding get it wrong?

A commonplace of theatre we have all
Heard is the unknown loitering in the wings
Who sweats on another's illness to be strong.
The frailty of genius is the call
That re-embodies the absent role and brings
To bated music a transfigured song.

Choose names to suit your taste. Well, the last reaches
And limits of the common world persist
(I'm ready for the screeches
Of protest — I know, it's nonsense to suppose
They still survive, like thinking ghosts exist
Or saying you believe in UFOs,
The Bermuda Triangle) with tales of creatures,

Not yetis, something of a humbler size,
A human image, Neanderthalers, say,
Peering from Caucasian woods, by a lake
In central Asia, in China loping away
Into hills; stooped in surprise
Beside a dozing scientist who'll wake
To meet his memory in thoughtful eyes,

Or dodging panic-fired shots and gone.
Nonsense. But like a premonition it stirs
Some sense of awe to think such beings move
On our perimeter, in the wings, to don
Like clothes roles that were ours and speak our verse
If, for whatever reason, we should prove
Unable to go on.

In Search of Time to Come

There's not much noise above the sputtering fire.
They don't speak much.
The children are settling to a private croon,
Though the baby whimpers, palping blindly to clutch
At a breast. Farther back, picked out by a
Final index finger of the sun, someone squats.
They'll be changing their abode quite soon,
No doubt.
The time requires a tacit finishing touch,
From women working at rough pots
And men scraping a hide to peg it out.

This mood, this life, is like a circle, turning
Always back
On itself: expectation interlocking
Ritual; impulse to novelty, for lack
Of its not yet invented learning,
Subsiding again to things that they take pleasure from.
A hum. A mother's body rocking.
They are, you would say, at home.

Only the cave mouth, that changeable screen,
Opens a gap
In the circumference; and when the light
Is gone, they have no words by which to trap,
Or the notions by which words could mean,
What that black window's showing for them to detect,
As they look, perplexed, into the night
And stare,
Then turn towards each other's bodies to tap
Their comfort. Someone, they suspect,
Is out there; and they're right. We are out there.

A World of Sense

Before glasses cleared the air
How many eyes, I wonder,
Not quite blind,
Read the world as a blur
Naturally, not guessing even that sight
For others was a matter less ambiguously defined
Than theirs, like sticklebacks
Whose lenses, chocked with parasites
From birth, are a seething of worms,
Kaleidoscopic focus,
Shifting forms.

Imagine, then, failings of the other senses,
Those, not deaf,
Whose hearing is like an ancient vase
Restored from odd pieces,
A construction of what is largely missing, whose music
Is more rests than notes; those
With (is it possible?) myopia of touch
Where "sure" is "in hand" and probing fingers
Send their nervous message,
When burnt, scratched, overreached,
Of tepid sludge.

Like guests at large in an ill-lit
Unknown house at evening
They'd make their way in the world,
Except they'd think it right,
Familiar, finding in mirrors old masters,
New harmonies in the plumbing, on mould-
Soft panels tapestries.
On this ground they would put up stern
Elaborate faiths, pronounce
The most specific heresies,
Exquisite punishments.

A pygmy, encouraged from the walled-in
Closeness of jungle which deprives
His people of perspective, was brought

To a wide hill, shown
The view. "What are those insects?" he enquired,
Pointing not far from his feet.
His guide scanned the ground
For ants, beetles, then shifting his focus
Saw the wildebeest
Swarming on the plain where that hand
And his smile faced.

Et in Arcadia Ego

Stropping her shoulderblades
On exercise,
Lean as the reaper of northern art,
The cheetah glides with a mechanical ease
Through shifting perspectives of the herds.

But their nervous motion too
Is mechanical
Merely, instinctive, and for now they have
No fear, as though sensing when a hunger will
Impel her and when not. She's like your shadow

Or the grass rising into place
When a foot
Is lifted, taking back its shape.
Their young frisk in the sunlight
Where she passes or must pass.

When she strikes their orchestrated terrors
Rip
The plain, drag down air like a hanging,
With that formal indignation at what can't be helped
Posed by a tragic chorus.

So they subside and mill
About the carcass
And the feast, grazing mildly by that shock
Of red, as if nothing more assertive than grass
Could arrest their ambling circle.

Division of Labour

The mantis strains in its new skin
To shed its younger body's slough
Which, unprepared to be cast off,
Clings like a smaller, weaker twin.

Both pale and tethered by a thread,
For just a moment they belie
What was divided here and why.
The living insect lies as dead,

Exhausted. The shell, empty, clear,
Accepts the breeze and moves again,
As though alive, and starts to strain
To break the tie that holds it here.

Dr Rogers' Report

A Letter from the New World

I

Its centre peaked with a volcanic chain,
Costa Rica falls from its divide,
Three-forested, each one a new domain:
La Selva on the Caribbean side;
Then Monteverde which clouds bathe and hide;
The third by the Pacific. The best place
To start, I thought, would be La Selva. I'd
Been there before. And now I could retrace
The lush diversity locked in that narrow space.

II

I saw again the moss-grown sloths and monkeys,
The frogs, all psychedelically designed
In colours elsewhere seen on racehorse jockeys.
On mist-hung Monteverde fog defined
The gnarled and twisted trees, their branches twined
With moss and epiphytic plants. Through haze
The bird whose plumage Aztec kings would bind
In coronals, the Quetzal, caught what rays
Of sun burned through, and flamed in metal-green displays.

III

At dawn the howler monkeys raised the sun,
Naming their name, macaws took scarlet flight;
The toucans' forms, grotesque enough to stun,
And butterflies bewilderingly bright,
Spectacular flowers in the forest light,
Arrayed themselves. The trees went to extremes.
Where midday cooled me spiders fished at night.
And crayfish eyes, responding with pink gleams,
Surprised my passing torch along the jungle streams.

IV

I flew from Costa Rica in mid-March
To Venezuela, bought a four-wheel drive.
Heat and no rain had left the country parched,
So dry you'd think that nothing could survive.
What streams were left drew everything alive
To choke their muddy chain of pools. And here
Capybara families came to dive
And drink, herons and ibises would spear
Piranhas captive to the dwindling area.

V

I stayed at Rancho Grande, a hotel
Deserted in the mountains by the coast.
At night its echoing corridors would fill
With bat wings. Just the place to shoot a ghost
Film or a thriller! But I was more engrossed
In the forest's drama — lianas, vines alight
With orchid sprays, frogs carrying a host
Of tadpoles on their backs, crabs (at this height!),
Nightmoths and insects dazed in multicoloured flight.

VI

Colombia was car trouble. In each town
An engine under the bonnet would amaze
Mechanics, who would then have to lie down
Or rope in locals, vagrants, for a day's
Discussion. On high roads, after these delays,
I travelled in low gear and disbelief
As machos passed on hairpin curves to graze
The crosses where their friends had come to grief.
And so I entered Ecuador with some relief.

VII

My goal was the Galapagos; to see
Darwin's Islands would have to be the aim
Of any who love natural history.
The birds and animals were all so tame! —
The blue-webbed gannets, orange crabs like flame,
Iguanas, the piratically black-
Bannered frigate birds. I snorkelled through a game,

Or ballet, with a stick among a pack
Of sea lions, reef fish our kaleidoscopic claque.

VIII
Ecuador was splendid. Discovered oil
Meant access roads constructed eastward to
The Amazon. In daylight you could toil
Up mountain passes whose surrounding view
Was all snow-capped volcanoes, and back through
Forested slopes to humid jungle night.
The roadsides were an orchid avenue,
Reds, yellows, muted mauves. Prismatic flight
Of butterflies upon the banks was a delight.

IX
Driving through patchwork Indian fields or arid
Lava-plains below the volcanic snows,
I headed southwards to Peru now, carried
By a road where no sane person ever goes,
The Inter-American Highway, in the prose
Of guidebooks fittingly described as being
"Terrible and little used". Up to my nose
In water, jeep awash at one point, seeing
Road turn into river, I couldn't help agreeing.

X
Immediately ensued a torrid hour
Or more of questioning and checking by
A customs man, who met me with a sour
Smile like a slice of lemon, sure that I
Was smuggling something in. They classify
Peru as "costa, sierra, selva" — band
Of coast, mountain backbone awesomely high,
And jungle. The coastal strip is sweeps of sand,
A desert fringe, huge dunes (say, twenty miles) and

XI
The barren ranges where a vulture stationed
In the wind is often the only sign

Of life. These ranges give no intimation
Of splendours offered by the Andes, spine
Of South America, till they decline
Eastward into jungle. I spent two weeks
At thirteen thousand feet where dawns define
Glaciers, fluted ice-cliffs, rock walls, peaks,
All backed by brilliant sky and mirrored in glass lakes.

XII
One valley here contained a plant that has
To be earth's most spectacular, they call
Puya Raimondii, a macelike mass,
Eight feet across, of barbed spikes in a ball,
Out of which a flaming candle, all
Pale green blossom, surges up and towers
Above the ground, thirty or so feet tall,
Nectar on tap from twenty thousand flowers
That a swarm of Andean Hillstar hummingbirds devours.

XIII
Driving across the Andes in this place
Was to see a grandeur frightening in scale,
My jeep advancing at an insect's pace,
Spinning on valley walls its threadlike trail.
Should you grow weary, your attention fail —
Instant disaster. Once, my back wheels skimming
Left me balanced midair, sweating and pale.
The contrasts stunned me: one day, wind and gleaming
Ice; next day, shrill cicadas, heat and parrots screaming.

XIV
I went to two reserves: the first, Paracas
Where, south of Lima on the desert shore,
Seabird colonies in their normal fracas,
Sea lions and fur seals abound. Condor
Country. I'd seen a few of them before,
Too far to photograph. Here, two immense
Birds regularly patrolled. I watched them soar
Above cliffs, outstretched in their magnificence,
Utterly overwhelmed by the experience.

XV

Further inland, high up in the "puna"
Grasslands, lay the second reserve that had been
Created specially for the vicuña.
I remarked how few staff members I had seen.
"Yes. Some terrorist bomb threat. They all seemed keen
To go, staff and police."! I wonder why?
Still, I stayed on for morning's unchanged scene:
Lakes rimmed with ice to greet the dazzled eye,
Flamingo flocks deep pink against a slatey sky.

XVI

I headed southwards steadily now, as
I travelled through the Andean plateau
And past Lake Titicaca to La Paz.
Bolivia was total chaos, though.
I was frustrated there, anxious to go,
And two months work and driving were a drain
On energy and enthusiasm. So,
Uncertain what results I might obtain,
I turned towards the Yungas, forests due for rain.

XVII

The road's spectacular: down valley walls
With huge drops to the gorge below, a lace
Of track through untouched cloud-forest, it falls,
Balanced on the narrowest passing place,
Eleven thousand feet or more in the space
Of fifty miles. And then the staggering
Extravagance of butterflies to face
After descent: confetti-clouds of wing-
Rise, camouflaged or advertised, were dizzying.

XVIII

Across the Altiplano by a road
Of doubtful standard (which, of course, I chose)
Onward to Chile. Fierce winds here erode
A lunar landscape. At last a road sign shows
My awesome destination: Santiago's
Two thousand kilometres on. Here lies

The Atacama desert. Nothing grows.
Nothing. Nothing. Nothing. Distance replies
Horizon on horizon to your beggared eyes.

XIX

Day's heat mirage gives way to dawn's soft greys,
Its subtle pinks, rusts, purples. And in turn
Desert gives way to farming. My midday's
Halt finds cherries and peaches, roadsides burn
With foxgloves, alstroemerias. I earn
My rest in Puerto Montt, almost the end.
But I've one passion left before return —
To visit Patagonia where bend
The stiff-winged arcs of albatrosses in the wind.

XX

My destination was Torres del Paine.
Here nature managed, just when I had thought
My sense of awe exhausted, to attain
Her wildest and most breathtaking: the wrought
Pink granite pinnacles and sharp cliffs caught
In cloud, the thwarted trees wind forced awry,
Ripped plumes of spray that wind and lake surface fought
For; and above it all the matchless, high
Serenity of condors circling in the sky.

Pedder

The shadow in the surf that empties beaches;
The drowned bell in a western bay
Clanging on the hinge of a grey
Tide: it is something in water that invests
Power in distortion, teaches
The threatened senses it arrests
What things in thin air are too frail to say.
The banners of a slaughter-
Wasted army heave in the slow lake water

More largely than in winds that threw them over.
A launch above the flooded lake
Extends the feather of its wake,
Brushing peaks. This is vertigo. I ride
Where the sky was and cloud cover.
Below, like air, the currents slide
Down hills and slur through filmy trees to make
As clouds would on the sand
Viscous shadows where the wrested myrtles stand.

Indo-European

I
Garrulous metastasis
Riddling the silent crafts,
Teaching them to talk about themselves
And swell with all the arts of rhetoric.

Unique surprise
For ancient birds, beggared
Thereafter by an alien lyric
That must name woods
It filled, specifically, tree by tree.

Prolix evolution
From a one-celled cry
Ahing its own echo
To polysyllabic monsters
Explicating at exhaustive length
Ponderous aetiologies of delight.

II
From such inarticulate beginnings
So much to talk about.

From such numberless offerings of the world
Arrayed to receive their own identities

All these glossaries in limbo
Desperate for an object to be meant by.

A mere few hundred words
At first, sounding out this gift

Called speech, learning the trick
Of conversation, their future living;

Syllables simply strung, like beads,
Consonant, vowel, consonant, vowel,

No clusters to confuse the novice
Tongue; the sounds a bit rigid,

Mostly stops, the looser pleasures
Of the fricative a discovery yet in store.

One language of a scattered tribe
Too naïve to name itself.

III

Now we fill pages
With symbols for the sounds. The languages
Have covered half the earth.

The dictionary's so big
It's lost count, a catalogue
Of meaning no mouth

Could ever make sense of.
Just like the fed five
Thousand's miraculous meal

A little bread and fish
Proved able to accomplish,
Leaving the baskets full,

What dropped from a few lips like crumbs,
Modestly expressed, now crams

The throats of millions and is not exhausted,
Or lost for words from what is wasted.

The Masked Ball

Unkind distortions with their faces skewed,
Like flounder heads, both eyes squashed to one side
And staring from the frame
Averse and mad and wide,
Characters in cartoons
Emit their messages. The jokes extrude
Sealed in balloons
As though to say "within this line another game

With other rules applies
Which is at once perspicuous and covert".
It's all at one remove,
Like a scientist who tries,
Experimenting in a vacuum, to prove
Something about the world but yet not of it.

Sole-eyed the living speakers float ideas.
They can't tell simply what they meant to mean,
Nor can they face each other
With what they would have seen.
The stranger's wanted street
Wearies direction. Confession interferes
With tea. A discreet
Smile has to satisfy the dream-articulate lover.

Their words drift roundly by
To burst in dazzling rumours. The earth becomes
A stage where the stunned crowd
Gapes at myths and the sky
Is lit with riddles. Like magic, lies concoct a loud
Rumbling in the hills and the valley hums.

At the masked ball all fantasy's excused
And facts are made up for. Personae nod
And smile with gold panache,
Lines marshalled like a squad,
And no-one dares to start
At the livid face beneath, the mouth that's used
To fall apart
Unspeakably. The room is charged with words that flash

As bright as masks, a script
A genius might have written which, when heard,
Suspends all disbelief,
But who, at home and stripped
Of his pen, is a bore, stammers, wears a private grief,
And never says a memorable word.

Now

The weather says it:
When clouds like swollen sponges
Take up the sky,
Staining the windows grey,
Blanking the mountain
Like news from a censored letter,
And rain is nailed
Home to secure the exits;

Or when it's blue
And hard as a kitchen tile,
Heat framing the town
Like a window, doming the house,
A bell jar emptied
And sealed against the air;

All now, it says,
Nothing is possible
But this, all here
And all immutable.

So illness, love,
The mindless head, the useless
Limbs that leave you
To become the place you lie in,
The woman who recurs
Like an echo, one
Word you go on mouthing
That must mean you.

Each second's tick
Is a drop of time bleeding
From the future.
Striking chimes fall plumb
Like a portcullis,
Leaving nowhere to pace

But the present hour
Which draws you out at last
From the tower clock,
As Einstein prophesied,
In still extension
That says now for ever.

Last Things

Enough to wind the clock
When time's familiar.
The spring's tension
Will carry out the hours
Mindlessly enough,
If not quite painlessly.

The traffic will seek out
Its destination,
Reasonably enough.
The labelled roads
Were put there just for this.
Movement was called for
And the space was filled:
Those little faces
That have grown and gone,
Those polished surfaces,
Set pieces of the table,
Those pictures that became
A field of vision,

That other face that watched
From the opposite chair
And also now is gone.

The space was filled
Without thought, without notice.
What concentration now
Will restore that concord
Of events and objects?

The shadow-driven cars
Still beleaguer
The highways as the sun
Divides itself amongst them
For the night, each one urged on
Across the window's space
By the formal twist
Of a hand on the clock's key.

It says, forget judgement,
Forget heaven and hell,
Small things, the tried diversion
Of an ignorant fear.
Death, yes, will be there
But the other three were here
Already, all along,
Unthought, unnoticed,
Waiting on such sorrow
And lost purpose.
Darkness, silence, nothing,
Each night now they return
And will return
With a patience that bespeaks
All the time in the world.

Slow Motion

Down the line
Continuously added to
The new cars shine
And move to a completion,
As monitored from above, that drives them off
In perfect time. Slow motion.
Faced with each car at the same stage
Passing, the worker at his station
Can gauge
No change, no movement,
But fixed attendance in a fixed design.

It's like a child two
People love. The constant one
Fails to construe
As altered a growth that locks
Its progress to her own. The distant one
Who seldom sees her wakes
With panic to a change that's exiled
Him in absence. As he looks
The child
Is borne away
From attachments once undone and now untrue.

So shoppers rise
Towards a higher floor, and back
Again crosswise
Those from above descend.
The interlocking steps take on their shift
Of passengers one end
Without disruption and without
Disruption at the other turn
Them out,
Like finished products.
Slow motion. Its impulse forwards, yet it plies

The same ground, night
And day, perfect with practice. Stood
There with feet quite

Still, its progress theirs,
They might abstractedly forget they're going.
But drawing in the gaze
Will show what's passing as they climb
And sink. One checks his watch. But this is
The time.
He's thought of something,
Looks back, but is carried onwards out of sight.

Over the Hill and Far Away

Barbed wire tells the limit.
A conifer,
Inveterate boxthorn, some small
Pale dusty pelargoniums
No harshness makes suffer,
Annoy the dreary summit

Of the cemetery's hill with persistent green.
Erosion,
Like an archaeologist, has marked the site
And got down to digging. A landslip
Where the graves were unrolls its confusion
Into paddocks. There's even a sign.

Well, to see spelt out
Like this
So plain an interdiction
Might trouble the faithful, but there it is:
The edge we may not pass
Crumbling before our feet,

The land that slips away from the very
Point
Of our decisions, taking its people like dissidents
In the night no official will find
Trace of, though there's always a patient
Queue. End of story,

And page by page or guessing ahead
We have
To read it. A snapshot will tell
The whole plot like an open book:
To the right the riddled hill half
Turns its good side;

Before the lens, arrested in departure,
The mother
Stares in black to acknowledge her taker;

Some steps behind, approaching
In blues and self-absorption, the daughter
Is eyeless in blown hair;

His face thrown upward to the wind's,
Yards
Away with eyes squeezed shut,
The grandson in red, summoned
From his distance, is running, running towards
The place where the picture ends.

The Tripwire

What could his thoughts have been that morning when
He woke, if he had slept, to this his last
And longest? The question, even in the asking,
Takes all its words away, and their reply,
Like an electronic sign escaping round
A building.

Damiens, the regicide,
Was led before an audience whose cheers,
We may be sure of it, were rapturous
In anticipation. His joints were drawn
And snapped, muscles ripped out with hooks, his flesh
Was gashed and peeled, with boiling tar and sulphur
Poured in the wounds, his belly opened up
And his own offal force-fed back to him.
He was torn apart by horses. All the time,
"Sweet Christ, dear Christ," he whimpered, while a priest
Scraped in attendance like a sycophant.

To give themselves away so blatantly!
Was it subtlety or simply love of pain
To drag his life so slowly out of him,
Or, rather, drag him away from his own life
And keep him living witness of his body's
Dismantling till they'd reached the heart of it?
The king being God's anointed, regicide
Becomes at once treason and heresy,
A crime against the state, a sin against God.
Punishment of the body, in this light,
Is nothing to the damnation of the soul.

They thought, you understand, they dealt in souls.

And now I seem to sense a thin and taut
Highpitched appalling intellectual scream,
Beyond the range of hearing, like a dog
Whistle, but making every nerve raw-edged,
That stretches out to meet this dead procession.
This is the tripwire where the judges fall

Arse over tip, bishops and cardinals
Sprawl headlong and their robes are smeared with blood,
Till their pronouncements and their pieties,
Formal and chill as letters carved in marble,
Bubble between their teeth through gore and muck.

We learn these days that even as we tell
Our daily lies some small twitch of the body
Also speaks to betray the fact: the eyes
Averted from an interlocutor,
The lick of lips, cleared throat, adjusted cluff,
The crossing and uncrossing of a leg.
While Damiens's body screamed its agony,
Though Damiens himself showed shocking restraint,
They too, his judges, true embodiers
Of righteousness and otherworldliness,
Which form a structure somehow kept aloft
Only by never looking at it straight,
Said what they did not say, condemning him,
And tripped and, falling, brought down on their heads,
Blind as Samson chained to his own undoing,
The edifice of the immortal soul
And its ascendancy.

Like toddlers who
Dabble, uninhibited, in their own shit,
Chattering as they do it, angel-faced,
The pious ones sing world-renouncing praise
With features set to show they've quelled all sense.
But as they kneel, their hands unconsciously
Range through this body opened to the world
And sticky fingers press the forbidden parts.

Jogwatch

First day of the new
Dispensation will be a joy.
Up so early for duty
To touch with an almost coy
Pride the patrol car's
Bright duco and chrome,
Buff them up a bit
With a casual sleeve and, in a dream,
Load lovingly the tools
Of the trade, finger the controls;
Then, with a nod, get in —
Gloved driver and the other one.

Sleek as a lone shark
In grey waters the car
Will nose the dawn light
Along favoured streets. And there
He'll be, the lucky first.
Tricked out in red —
Singlet, shorts, sneakers —
Feeling the flush of blood
Rise to the surface of his skin
As he breathes smugly, he'll turn
The corner, the happy twit,
And run bang up against it.

Best to aim for a knee
First, or a shoulder, to bring
Him down but still aware.
You'll want him conscious to prolong
The pleasure. Then, as he lies
Groaning, uncomprehending,
Give him a nudge in the balls
To concentrate his mind and, bending
Over with a smile, flash
The Jogwatch badge, push
The barrel hard against his face
And plug the sod for the *coup de grâce.*

Ah, the first morning
Will be a joy. Yes,
There'll be a few changes.
But joggers are not, of course,
Alone on the list. Oh no!
All health freaks
Will have to go; youths
In lairy wagons or on bikes
(Well, any adolescents);
Readers of Vogue (and glossy
Mags in general); Mormons,
Other fanatics, I daresay
(Well, any churchgoers);
Lefthanders; redheads;
Owners of Alsatians (Alsatians),
Keepers of caged birds
(Well, any pets) and . . .

Late Thoughts in the Greek Camp

The mighty shadows flap, bully and liar,
Rippling between the night wind and the fire
On the tent walls; their figures sway and flower
Over the flames and over us who cower
Agape, hanging on their squabble, like small
Boys watching bigger brothers in a brawl.

But I've blocked out their shouting since he spoke,
Thersites, it's his words I hear — not the choke
And blubber he's making now for the swift blow
Odysseus fetched him with his sceptre, no,
But his outburst earlier, that hornet's sting
Of a speech that shocked us all, still echoing
Around my head. No wonder they shut him up
So quick. Plain talk like that could put a stop
To this charade of theirs for good.

Disaster's
Threatening to engulf us and our masters,
With perfect sense of timing (and with manners
That would stink in the company of tanners,
Though they can scorn Thersites as a churl)
Are bickering about who gets a girl
To bed. What are the odds for me whose will is
Stronger? and whether it turns out Achilles
Or Agamemnon leaves his mark on her?
I'm still left with a hand for comforter.
I can't decide whose lunacy is worse:
These lords of ours who bandy curse for curse,
Or we who sit obediently and hear
Them out, relishing every boast and sneer,
The cut and thrust of pride. Yes, all their lust
Will come down to for us is cut and thrust.
Our bodies are their shields. We risk our necks
And they get all the money and the sex.
This whole thing's just an exercise for them.
We're caught up in a separate stratagem.
They haven't come for Helen. There's a rumour
That the lady, who must have a sense of humour
If it's true, and is clearly much too clever

For us, jumped ship in Egypt, and so never
Got this far at all, never got to enjoy
The climate we know all about at Troy.
But this would make no difference to our lords.
They need the practice with their spears and swords,
Somewhere to model their equipment and
Impress each other in a foreign land.
They know what they are fighting for. They measure
Honour by the chariotful of treasure —
Oh, and flesh.

Ten whole years here I've been blinded.
I see now that my lords are feeble-minded.
The outcome of the war, let well alone
Our welfare, is a poor second to their own
Private competition. Are Trojan senses,
I wonder, as removed from Trojan princes?

I fear the Gods can't love us. How could they
Have faith in leaders who behave this way?
Or if they do, then they are fools as well,
Not worth our worship. Maybe this is hell:
We sit here in the night — will sit, have sat —
Our futures forfeit for a princes' spat.
Awed by their fathomless stupidity
We watch their antics but are neither free
To speak nor go away. The dark swift ships
Lie idle like the tongues behind our lips
And look to home. No word of ours will put
Them out to sea, and I doubt that I'll set foot
In Greece again. The mighty shadows flap,
Between the wind and fire, a shifting trap,
Flap emptily and emptily we gape,
Shamed, hopeless, without power or escape.

Chess

Gold-hampered watcher of intrigues beneath
Him, he treads the two brief chambers of his rule.
(Elsewhere, oblique, sun on an altarpiece
Shadows a mitred head, a proffered jewel
And lips. Its way cleared by complexities,
A mounted blade cuts like a precise tool.)
But his low-voiced consort has the world on lease
And death takes letters from her yellowed teeth.

So battlemented hills in evening light
Debouch dark columns with an edge like frost
And fields are emptied under other walls
Where screams appeal for morning and are lost.
So regal laughter eats the distant halls
And a crowned head, eyeless now, sees out the night.

Rapunzel

Silence now again. The table's cleared,
The meal itself the usual contest
With silence to see who first
Will break, like one outstared,
Relinquishing the impulse to find words
At all.
Combing its yellow out through trees and clouds
The rising moon floats up above the wall,
Though that sight isn't dared.

Odd interchanges of the ordinary,
Of course, still punctuate the hours — as few
As they can cater to
Between the dusk when he
Gets back and the time the first retreats to bed —
Though never
The urgencies of which both could show need
If only they knew how, who would have the other
Blank to this long dismay.

So she settles by the lamp's hair-yellow glow,
Her lap arranged with fabrics, needles, wool,
To embroider trivial
Ornaments she will stow
And forget in cupboards, or to darn and mend
By the hand's
Mechanical remembrance while her mind,
Having its mechanisms too, stamps, grinds
Out its repeated Oh,

Its ache for that small smiling form, years lost,
Though not one detail lessened by the years
Of absence, the hooked years,
Empty and gone to waste
Like her embrace. He stoops to disturb the fire
And feels
The swirl of heat around his face like hair,
Or sits pretending to hone a blade he trails
On a stone that isn't moist,

Or else will fashion yet another haft
He knows he cannot need for months, while his mind
Yaws, swinging out of hand
Like his daily axecraft,
Though never able to cut through the knot
Of nothing,
The pressure on his palms, the cradle's weight
He passed to those hooked hands, sharp and scathing
As holly leaves, and left.

When she sighs, crumpling cloth from her rising lap,
That she thinks she'll go to bed now, it's to drown
Her inner accusation:
"Coward! Fool! Witch's dupe!
Your promise!" When he grunts he'll not be long
What can
This mean but "stupid woman with your craving!
Did you think that she, robbed of her rampion,
Would let your own escape?"

She pauses by the door and her eyes ache back.
He stays his hand a moment from its cramp
And lifts his head. Moon, lamp
And fire stream round them like
The long entangling loops of yellow hair
Lowered
To catch their every look and bitter hour
And wish and memory since. She turns to bed.
His eyes drop to his work.

Sleeping Beauty

About you like a hall of mirrors shone
Their smiling niceness, turnkey approval which
Was welcoming you at last (so soon)
Into what would lock like an iron gate
Behind you, be your world.
Strange then that in this rich,
This gaudy festival that swirled
Around
You like the whirlpool where you might be drowned
Your presence after all was too sedate
To notice now. None of them would
See you, not one.
Amid so much glass, though, you were bound
To be broken up and lost and theirs for good.

You left the hall of mirrors and slipped out
Unnoticed from the braying celebration
In which your life, without a doubt,
Had been, you saw now, slept away so far.
The choice you hadn't guessed
Before, an anticipation,
Drew you lightly off in quest
To explore
The passageways that must have waited for
Your taking, always. Like a faint hurrah
Or protest (too far off to care)
The revel's shout
Was swallowed in your now confessed
Excitement as you turned for the spiral stair.

She was there as you expected, solemn-faced,
Pale and beautiful, calling to your mind
One . . . but all this was being erased,
Withdrawing now from substance like the haul
Of a swimmer from the shore
By the insistent bind
Of undertow. This choice, then, or
Where else
To go? For even here, at the castle's
Most secretive extent, all ways met wall.

Your finger inched for her device
(No words to waste;
Eyes locked with eyes, you bartered smiles)
And shivered to the spindle's kiss of ice.

And as you slumped, there briefly welled, then hung
In stasis round you like a frozen wave,
Their distant laughter's chilling song,
Smiling niceness, turnkey approval which
Had welcomed you in trust
To teach you to behave,
In the hall of mirrors you were just
On the point
Of slipping from unnoticed.

The Pied Piper

The doors shut to the street when women hear
My passing, or the crooked hint
Of my approach.
Faces withdraw from windows when I veer
Into view, and talking groups fold in
Upon themselves like flowers at dusk, falling silent.
They don't know how to see me anymore.
Past them I limp and lurch
And wait to hear the murmur start again.

Oh but I hear the voices from inside,
In hidden yards, of those too young
To follow, and
So saved. I see the women too parade
The swollen bellies they still hope
Will take the place of ghosts that even now they cling
To. Clip-clip, like a dripping pipe or dead
Twig's tap at a pane, my sound
Disturbs the cobbles they pretend to sweep.

Soon enough they settled on me the cost
That should be his, and think that's me
Accounted for.
And they would rather I too had been lost,
Not to suffer (but they do)
Dealings with the price of their own parsimony.
Like someone with no memory I exist,
But neither now nor here,
And have to wait on them to make me true,

To remember what they know but can't confess,
Dream of but only half believe.
Sometimes it seems
I see a coloured cape or sleeve swung loose
Among a crowd, or slip from sight
Around a corner. Breathless with contempt I strive
For the spot, but there is no-one there of course.
And then when the wind comes
That way, I watch the Koppelberg and start

To hear old piping and young voices, have to
Hobble to their source, knowing the breeze
Will drop or change
Before I'm even halfway there, time after
Time. Weeds in the Weser among rocks
Shadow sleek bodies, while the road climbs and disappears,
Like them in past games, mockery of the swifter
For the slow — slow to revenge,
And pity, for this worst of all their tricks.

Bluebeard's Castle

One

One palm to test the tenor of the wall,
A curve which turns aside each forward step,
Like a simple act in a dream you keep
Repeating, that won't go as you wish it, no,
But strays away obliquely to your will,
Threatening. A glow, two windowed balconies
That give a light some tastes might fancy as
Intimate, quiver like water on the wall.
Slowly I see them as I glide between
Chambers, in the same repeated circle.

* * *

Again as it once was, the exclusive view
From the upper windows on which laughter would,
At times, from the favoured group, thud like a gust
To punctuate the silent tableau he
Was centre of, or rather silent film
I mooned at like an adolescent struck
By an idol, synchronizing fantasy
To the screen's mute conversation between lips.
Quite separate, the blown voices braced my face
Behind the dappled glass, like snatches of
An aria where melody plays upon
The sentimental urges that we turn
Secretly to scenes of fulfilment, the words
Music-eaten. Who knows what's being sung?
Lives are concocted on a mere effect,
An accidental pose or emphasis.
You give yourself into a stranger's keep
Who might be anything.

The favoured group. I wanted what it was
In him that drew them to him, thinking this
Was who he was and who I fell in love with.
I didn't know two people in their love
Invent two others who are never seen
By any person on this ghosted planet.

It happened, then, I wasn't so remote
As I had feared, nor he so favoured. So
It began, as all these passions do, the most
Unlikely merging of the disparate,
Come to seem inevitable. Even
Afternoons through disreputable suburbs,
Demolished rows, were like walks in privileged
Precincts where the held hand's a gratuity
Of too much feeling, not a politeness paid
Against a turned heel.

So much was said in that rush to confess
More than the other could, and so unburden
The pretence of fault that lovers take delight
In affecting, that I failed to notice
How little his expansive monologues
Delivered of himself or of his past.
And sometimes out of nothing, for no reason
I could identify, no mindless word
Of mine that might have stung him, he would thrust
Like a bayonet some mocking savagery,
Belittling bitterness like a reflex jab
Against a blow received. Wanting possession
He would not be possessed, that faculty
In him held by some old inveterate
Spectrum of events. The look from his eyes
Was like the livid spillage from a door,
Slightly ajar, behind which there recoils
A murderous silence.

Again as it once was, the distant view.
Living with him has now become again
A promenade in the estate before
The shuttered house, timetabled loitering
In the outer chambers of a stately home,
Where the unanswered questions, terminated
Speech, are the sashed-off corridors that lead
To private quarters, private habitudes.

And do I hear or do I just imagine
The grouped and wafting voices off, like laughter
From the attic that is never spoken of,
The study where the henchmen are in session,
Instructed in their contract? Or do those

Passages contain only vacant rooms
And echoes of his own talk with himself,
The episodes of an entailed bequest,
Reanimated by a closed communion?

Where shall I go? What will become of us?

Two

A greenish glow lent by the lower storeys
Laps like a pool around the central stairwell,
And gives a light some tastes might fancy as
Intimate. Two windowed balconies
Are quivering like water on the wall.
Slowly I see them as I glide between
Chambers, in the same circle that repeats
Itself. A faint resistance hushes past.
No corridor connects these plush apartments.
One room, as at Versailles, gives to the next.

* * *

If you could know, my love, now occupied
With evening's practices in other rooms,
Believing I'm oblivious — I who judge
Your every placement and activity
Just by the length of silence between sounds,
Enriching them, drawing the details from them
Like someone reading out of the bare score
A well-known music. That music playing now,
Like sympathetic magic, makes the sky
Richer than the time is, extending me
A spurious vigour from its century,
Reasonable and clear and full of life.
But when the music stops?

Oblivious! Look. The full moon on the harbour
Peers at the city like a left-out child.
As well say that the moon's oblivious
Of the sun. It makes no light, merely reflects
The sun though no sun's visible. And when
Light is eclipsed the moon is lost in the dark

Like a single homestead in the country night
That disappears when everyone goes to bed.

The wealth in other eyes you took for me
Is only their pretence, a fashioning,
A quality they flattered in themselves
In seeing me. I thought that I had found
In your remoteness, which wasn't subject to
That false allure, an understanding. But
Not so. Is it through a one-way glass that I
Look out and watch them watching in my form
What they imagine? Or is it the reverse
And what they turn their smiles towards is me
Who observe the glassy blindfold of myself?

Life, my love, is a gift like any other;
You have to have the talent to do it well.

Alone I scarcely feel that I exist.
Looking at others like the harboured moon
I see them from a distance or great height,
As if they're moving under water, all
Their gestures and expressions fearfully slow,
Distorted and deliberate as they
Swivel towards me their unhurried heads
That may not see.

Those noises, elongated and profound,
Impeded like a slowing 78,
Can surely not be speech. I can't explain
Myself to them. And even you, my love,
Who like a necromancer make these limbs
Work, these senses feel, do not draw speech
From me of what occurred before we met.
For should you come so near now as to learn,
Then like the moon's eclipse you would put out
Yourself and me, and we would never see
Each other, then, in your unlighted circle.
Stumbling in that blacked-out intimacy
Who knows what scenes you'd come upon, played out,
Oblivious, then, certainly, of you,
Except as you would suit their purposes
To incorporate your anonymity

Into their dangerous rehearsal, scenes
I'd not explain to you, being part of them.

Three

Slowly I see them as I glide between
Chambers, in the same circle that repeats
Itself, translucent shiftings of a form.
A faint resistance to my face sighs past.
No corridor connects these plush apartments.
There are no doors. One room gives to the next
Room, but each is as though I haven't moved.
One palm to test the tenor of the wall,
A curve which turns aside each forward step,
Like an act in a dream you keep repeating.

* * *

Those early days seemed all spent out of doors,
Munificence of the emotions irked
By decorum and the hedged propriety
That walls and ceilings counselled. They put on
An expansive habit, outwardness, display,
The egoistic flaunting all think new
And memorable, worthy of the world.
Or so it felt to her. And she imagined,
In his silence, that it was so for him
Too. In new days exploratory passion
Needed new territory for settlement.
Afternoons through disreputable suburbs,
Demolished rows, were like walks in privileged
Precincts. In parks they'd never visited
Before, they'd lie, getting drunk on little
Enough, blind in the sun, rubbing spilt oil
Into bare feet, or on the back of a hand
With a lagging finger. What was happening?
What subtext in the fulsome autumn light
Was prompting words a fraction of a second
Before the wetted lips began to move,
And urged the angle of the knee or chin,
How far the hand should open, where be placed,
Intensity of gaze, the eyes' dilation,

A mindless acquiescence while the mind
Looked elsewhere like a bribed custodian?
But into that assent of appetite,
As quick to learn its movements as a child
Pressing a nose or finger to its mirrored
Twin, nothing could be read of motive, whether
Commitment or a mummer's tutelage.
So she, interpreting his readiness
As counterpart to hers, would not suspect
His giving might be just a passive ploy,
A refusal to receive held to contain
Involvement, making her vision of the day
An intricate illusion, like an Escher,
An idea without referent, like the sound
Of one hand clapping. Perhaps it suited him
That this largesse was in a neutral region
Where show might be enough.

A headland southward of the louring city
He *had* been to before, they drove to once,
And strolled along the bluff incongruously
Where fishermen cast their lines for rock cod,
Blackfish, in waters that were smoking round
The sandstone juts like flames eating a log,
As though the ground they stood on were encircled,
Closing in. He showed her over the rocks
To the pebbled inlet and the malign pool
Secreted halfway up the hill, too high
For tides to rinse, like a polluted tarn
Seeped into by the hillside, a brooding calm
Harbouring all the horrors of a childhood's
Reading, drawing them to the edge to trail
A stick in the soupy fringes, or let plop
A rock thickly farther out and wait for
Slow ripples to come labouring back to shore
Like a sluggish subaqueous echo.

Autumn still had its sting. They'd stop by trees
To kiss, caress each other, half frustrated
By the surrounding inhibition of
Preoccupied fishermen, half aroused
By that same presence, laughing off instead
An unwilling lust. Perhaps it suited him
That love could be professed without enactment,

The motions gone through but the fact withheld
In passion plays on the outskirts of resolve,
The need exhibited but not conveyed
In the deed of gift that might lay claim to him.

Four

One palm to test the tenor of the wall,
A curve which turns aside each forward step,
Like a simple act in a dream you keep
Repeating, that won't go as you wish it, no,
But strays away obliquely to your will,
Threatening you. The wall turns me aside.
Am I asleep or, wakeful in the dark,
Do I take my house, domestic and familiar,
For some realm parallel where vision is
Foreshortened, time condensed, where atmosphere
And objects that obsess it are poignantly
Mere adjuncts to an irremediable
Mischance? A greenish glow from lower storeys
Laps like a pool around the central stairwell
And gives a light some tastes might fancy as
Intimate, enough to see by, storeys
Constructed by a puritanical
Perfectionist, where nothing is forgotten,
Nothing forgiven. Like a message taped
On an endless loop that keeps concluding back
To its beginning, there recur the shapes
Of violence, lived through and memorized,
Chastisement, rancour, murder done by heart,
Severed compassion, refusal to believe.

A faint resistance to my face sighs past.
No corridor connects these plush apartments.
One room, as at Versailles, gives to the next,
Where the Sun King strolling to his mistress's
Recline might master mimicry, observing
Successive couples shape their bodies to
The palpitating figment of his desire.
There are no doors. Either I am unreal
Or this place is, for I pass between the rooms
Through faint resistance hushing at my face.
But each room is as though I haven't moved.

Slowly I see them as I glide between
Chambers, in the same circle that repeats
Itself, translucent shiftings of her form,
Standing and looking, sadly? or with concern?
To understand? or knowing all too well?
The right hand, crescent, on the point of some
Admonishment or caress, the mouth perhaps
Shaping a reproach or flattery,
Simply, perhaps, a kiss — her lips, her head,
Cool and transparent like that Aztec skull,
Perfect in crystal.

A greenish glow, two windowed balconies,
Their membrane blinds lash-fringed and quivering
Like water on the wall. An ancient music,
Implicit in the circumstance, floats and
Forgets itself in one inventive phrase,
Permanently present, unrepeated.
My steps so slow like someone under water,
I strive in a rising panic, but too late;
Room after room wanting to welcome dawn
But never lit, multiplications of
That single body, a flicker of glassy light
At certain angles, eaten by the dark
At others, silent, poised, her beauty held,
Untouchable, unknown and dangerous.

Li Tsung-ping

The snow is deep about the tents
And Li Tsung-ping is bowing to the captain.

Autumn here is short.
Yesterday the birchleaves were like gold coins in the sun.
Today the snow is falling like a thousand years,
Blossom from a frozen tree.

Dersu said,
"An old Chinese walked by here yesterday."
"How can you tell he was Chinese?" we asked.
"By the print of Chinese boots."
"How do you know that he was old?"
"Old men always walk on their heels."

Heels deep in snow, he's walking away,
His body doubled under a huge pack.

Last night we meant to call him to the fire.
But Dersu said,
"Do not disturb him. His thoughts are far away.
He's remembering the blossom in his garden.
He's sixty-four now. Forty years ago
His brother stole his wife."

We came upon him huddled in the doorway of a hut.
When the captain offered food and drink
He started back, wide-eyed,
As though we were ghosts, his memories flesh and blood.

Now at dawn, the earth in frozen flower,
He's come to say goodbye.

The snow is deep about the tents
And Li Tsung-ping is bowing to the captain.

Futures

1 Labyrinths

What's waiting is in fact,
Unlikely as it seems,
Everything.
Only the many-faceted eye of an insect
Could hold all the futures that look down,
Like Homer's
Gods, for the mortal act.

The forks and turnings rise
Up from the path
Like mirrored feet.
The ghostly hedges of an omnipresent maze
Scrape every shoulder. The spectral stone
Of the labyrinth
Replays the same echoes

To each glum neophyte,
And none can tell
Who will feed
The Minotaur, who walk out
Alive to the hushed crowd and hurl the head
Of a bull
In the blind sunlight.

Merely by chance for some
The fatal turn's
Not taken.
For others comes the unimagined time
When, watching themselves like a gaoler at the door, they see
Their hands
Flexing at a handle in the gloom.

2 Destinies

Whose breathing
Beyond the partition
Follows even now
Your own breath's pattern?

Here, paper thin,
It could show a hand splayed,
Fine as a frog's foot,
Lightly on the other side.
A few steps and it wastes
To nothing or thickens like the Chinese wall,
Unyielding to a million fists.

That other,
Now near,
Now distant, may never
See you, die a stranger,
Or then again, quite
Unexpectedly tomorrow,
Where the wall vanishes like frost
In the sun, be there before you.
Whom you love more than living
Might have been as unimaginable
As the dream you woke before having.

Choices
Stand like a glass
Against the wall. It mirrors
This room, and your mirrored face
Watches with dismay the hand
Raised against it, then recedes
From your challenge. But over your shoulder,
Look, infinitely backwards,
A corridor of windows frames
Figures gesticulating in clear squares,
Not seeing you from all their rooms.

3 Sets

In a circle of acquaintance
Total strangers may have a friend
In common,
Enemies be equally attached
To one man or woman.
It brings to mind
The circles in Venn diagrams,
Intersecting and crosshatched
To show relations
Between different sets and terms.

The generations swell
And fall like breathing in a still room.
The long
Dead, old when I was born,
Draw me into the shaded ring
Of the past, as some
Not even born yet
Will mark me on their futures, linking what has been
With what will be, until
The circles break apart.

Machine Readable

Nesting, here, in cotoneaster by the window,
(It's a warm spring day)
Two sparrows, their riffling like the pages of my book,
Corner my eye. But it's not my shadow
Draws them to the pane, but they
Themselves. For the male,
Who sees himself as his own rival,
Flies at the glass on the attack,
Bringing closer him he'd ward
Away, and cannot stop, any more than cease
Reflecting at himself. This worries me.
I hate to see him made so helplessly
Disturbed, hard
Against the limits of his brief consciousness,

Butting like a clockwork toy
Which marches on the spot against the skirting.
I don't want to think that's how they live,
But see no other way.
Caterpillars, scouting
Head to tail
On a cup's lip, would keep their single
File, could they survive
That long, till Voyager plays out
Its puzzle of Bach to a distant quasar, and face
No alternative to what
Their nature lets them see, without recourse.

So. At night I lie in bed
And perhaps on this occasion
Cannot sleep. My mind like a three-year-old
Will not be still, but will range and gad
And make a different version
And plot and watch
Its plotting. Surely this, this fetch,
This ghost in the machine's not walled
By the shape of bone, eye, appetite.
But I want to sleep and I can't and it worries me. Helpless.

My mind can't stop reflexion
On itself, but flutters like those wings' distraction
Against glass at what
Its nature is to see, without recourse.

Tammy's Lover

Outside the window where his eyes are aimed,
Though dreams of Tammy leave them blind with love,
The bees go on as they were made to do,
Losing themselves in budding rose, foxglove.

Something, perhaps, in their mechanical hum,
Perfection of performance without thought,
Might have been food for his, but Tammy's on
His mind just now, reducing it to nought.

He's got the place refurbished, spick-and-span.
He's bought a bedspread for the double bed.
He reads (again!) the postcard Tammy sent
Him and her words have whited out his head.

But at last the day arrives. At last he hears
A longed-for vehicle pull up outside
And rushes out with open arms and cheque
To take possession of his precious bride,

Who, in the bedroom, he unwraps and lifts
Out of her box — a woman made in heaven
(That's what the label says, a *Heaven Products'*
Money-back guarantee you can believe in).

Computerized and robotized, oh Tammy,
Articulate for love's work, Tammy makes
All the right noises of encouragement,
The amenable few movements that love takes.

A cunningly placed on-switch sets in train
The intermittent batting of her eyes,
Her gentle thrust, while pressure activates
Her vocalizing program and she sighs.

What did Garance say? *C'est si simple, l'amour?*
Yes, love is simple. Child of paradise,
He can't believe that life offers so much,
And all for such a reasonable price.

Solution sweet. He's even moved to whisper
Sweet nothings in her ear. His passion seeps
Between her plastic thighs, on which one arm
Lies like a dead weight, moveless, while he sleeps,

Having drifted — though he's failed to switch her — off;
So as she stirs all night by his dreaming face
Her repertoire of moans says yes to air
And her blind eyes blink their thank-yous at blank space.

On First Misreading Robert Gray's "The Death of Ronald Ryan" as "The Death of Ronald Reagan" (February 3, 1967)

But this is appalling, far worse
Than I'd ever been led to suspect.
Am I the only one who's been in the dark?
Has the whole world been playing along all these years
Since he carked?

I'm trying to come to grips. I know,
The world's full of wonders, I pay due homage
To the unaccountable. But ghosts?
Still, it would explain the assassin's bullet, a direct hit
That went straight through him and caused no appreciable
damage.

No, no. Or a preservation job? They called in the team
That processed Mao, perhaps.
(Well, he *does* sleep a lot.) A touch of bionics on his joints
And Nancy or an aide (of course!) behind him
With an arm stuffed up his shirt to work his lips.

Or how about — some stunt man
From his movie days, a lookalike who shot
His tough scenes, roped in again
For duty? An actor president was bad enough,
But an actor's substitute?

Let's face it, whichever account is the truth,
Our fate's left looking pretty iffy.
Whether he turns out to be some Canterville Ghost, or a
Waxwork,
Or the stand-in who's thumped in the head and trampled by
horses,
It's cold comfort for me. I can't speak for Gaddafi.

My God. The 20th anniversary of his death not six months off
And he's still on the job. I need time to think.
Robert, please, give me some more information,
Give me a steadying hand,
Gimme a drink.

Ronnie: An Embarrassment in Three Groans

Groan the First: Simplicity Itself

As proof the US hasn't lost its nerve,
And countries get the leaders they deserve,
Lo! out of Hollywood by Reader's Digest
(And if this is a joke it isn't my jest)
Is born (and born again) a President
Who reveals the complex as self-evident,
Who can in just one intellect embrace,
Despite his years, ideas not out of place
Among schoolchildren. What a *tour de force*!
With foreign policy from John Wayne's horse,
Technology from Spielberg and Lucas,
(And both from Rambo), he vows the Reds'll nuke us
Over his dead body. This is good to hear.
It's reassuring that his Grand Idea
Can be explained in words a fool would know:
Like gee-gee, gee whiz, gaga and gung ho.

Groan the Second: Sleeper

The White House hums. The boys are on the go.
And hum's the word: they keep their talking low.
The loudest sound — a wristwatch going bleep.
It's only 9 o'clock and Ron's asleep.

Midmorning and the Oval Office waits
With embarrassed smiles. Aides stall with delegates.
The loudest sound — an index finger's tap.
Well, it's 11 and Ron needs his nap.

But here comes lunch. They eat as they confer.
Shultz with a mouthful hears a sort of purr.
A head of hair is level with the drinks.
Afraid so — Ron is grabbing forty winks.

Before the press, a kip; till dinner, a snooze;
A rest before one of those Falwell do's.
No, Jerry, that's not praying, that bowed head.
The poor man's tuckered out: lead him to bed.

There's no rest for the wicked, so he must
Be sleeping after all the sleep of the just,
And just may wake up one day to a cough
And "Sir, some bad news while you just dozed off."

Groan the Third: Oscar Khayyam

The moving picture shows; and, having shown,
Moves on: no matter how you laugh or groan
The past's played out. There are new films to make.
Well, so we may have thought. We should have known.

Step forward, Ron. You guessed it — he's the dude.
In any place or context Ronnie's cued
To coin a wisecrack, piety, *mot juste*,
Fresh from some 40s flick he played or viewed.

You thought only the Reds rewrote the past?
He leaves reporters speechless, aides aghast,
By citing wartime incidents they trace
To films in which he or his chums were cast.

Apotheosis of the American Dream,
A regular guy, a player on the team,
Who made the silver screen and White House too,
And can't tell which is which. "More! More!" they scream.

So here's to you, old troop-, er, trouper, Ron,
Whose moving picture stuck and can't move on.
A great act, but you'll miss the warm applause
When, with the wind, your audience is gone.

All Stock Must Clear

Naked mannequins wait,
Almost alive, for garments to display,
Almost, you'd say,
Appealing out of decency for dress.
Dummies, they neither call for nor create.
It is the clothing
Here that is on show.
The outfits come and go,
The models wear the changes, powerless.
But nothing comes of nothing.

Like energy which, it seems,
Can neither be created nor destroyed
But redeployed,
Transformed, so the projections of the mind
Are simply refashioned from the same stock themes.
Age-mirrored, wild
With memory, the son prowls
His backward house and howls,
But the poisoner, the parent he can't find
There, and the tainted child

Are interchangeable.
Sooner or later they will be the same
With their single name
And double time. Then room to room he'll hear
His own steps and a voice as terrible.
So rancour, guilt,
Desire or joys that flower
Like certain cacti, an hour
Or two in darkness and then disappear,
Are they summoned by or felt

For them who wait out there,
Appealing, his words, her ambiguous kiss?
Or, powerless
As mannequins, do they wear the changes? Just
As disturbed water will churn up to air
And unload wrack,

Finally all moods come
To mind and weigh on some-
One, rising like the old man from the dust
To cling to Sinbad's back.

Vikings

I
They're here. But they have heard of image now.
Asking for it, the brilliant city reeks
With impatience. They've disowned the dragon prow.
Ridiculous beards are stripped from shaven cheeks.
Blade folds to Parker, cape to pinstripe suit;
Conservatively they are dressed to kill.
And to think the place will buy back what they loot
And have them in and vie to do their will.

An empty frame's *Le Déjeuner sur l'herbe*;
A movement's silent in Tchaikovsky's Fifth;
The King's Men find the play a few lines short:
History. They've been acquired and won't disturb
The show. What's in a name? A surface bought.
Through the mall young artless GI Nazis drift.

II
They were like children, ruthless innocents.
They came on the tide of present appetite.
No more than a squalling toddler can make sense
Of a mother's time and wishes could they fight
Impulse, reflect upon the burning town —
The pillaged treasury, a sacrament
Despoiled, raped women or the men cut down.
They grabbed what glittered in the sun and went.

But what was worse? Havoc, the emptied land,
The corpsefire hill that watched the fading wake?
Or the year they came and stayed? Not in their going
But in persistence was the overthrowing.
The vanquished then forgot to understand
And gave their victors what force couldn't take.

III
Think of the Parthenon. A model's shown
Mounted before it in a gauche excess

Like a cosmetic on that marble bone.
The cachet they would market in her dress,
Lips, sightless scent, fades with each pictured laugh
Faster than in the wind. Her buyers trace
An empty hill in a glossy photograph
Saying "Parthenon" under a woman's face.

The merchants come and take and come and stay.
What's history but a glitter they can't resist
That's rubbed to nothing by their handling? They
Hold a mask that's paid for to be kissed,
Copied from one who doesn't look the same
And has disappeared; but they still make her name.

Metopes

Democratic and surprised divinities,
Plane travellers may see what was never seen,
A sort of inner sanctum, strange
As Tutankhamen's in the Valley of the Kings,
Hidden in open air: flauntings
Of the Cerne Abbas giant at the skies,
Horses disposed over chalk-etched
Hills; in Peru,
Hummingbird and monkey sketched
On the Nazcan plain that have only been
Ruts in the desert, but arrange
From a thousand feet a complex living wholeness,
Expressly, you might think, for a viewer's eyes.
No need to rope in spacemen, though, for this.
Well then, who?

Torrigiano's Henry and Elizabeth
Contain and offer, lying in bronze relief,
Such perfectness as can be shown.
Their figures, gilded bronze upon black marble base,
Like sure self-dreaming shadows, face
Above your eyes' view upwards into death,
Half seen behind their grille. Why make
Such effort for
The ceiling's sake? God? Perhaps. But take
The Greeks. Surely they'd long since lost belief
In theirs when they built the Parthenon,
But still went on pursuing an unmatched technique
For obsolete grotesques of early myth,
Occasions now for a tragic rhetoric.
What they hardly saw,

Ranged on the frieze above the colonnade,
Metopes displayed in their restraint and force
Perfection too high to be faced,
Like windows looking through themselves at what they are.
What am I saying? *L'art pour l'art?*
Perhaps, but there is more. For those who made
Them looked beyond in being bound,

Exceeded by
Means of what's completely found
Within, like a satellite's outreaching course
Turning into orbit. So placed,
Like all art holding back even what they're revealing,
These works show all you need to see. In aid
Of higher purpose God will do, a ceiling,
Or the empty sky.

Occupational Hazards

Arriving over Sydney, piercing the clouds'
Meniscus, like an insect through the surface tension
Of a pond,
We floated in a strange dimension,
The aqueous light
Of those few moments when the city swims,
Not yet quite real, not quite
Defined in its constituent parts — the glimpse
Of beach with its persistent crowds,
Firm landmarks and the free suburbs beyond —
But still somewhat awash, unclear
In the overlap of flight,
The blue and pointless hours that brought us here.

So amid the tiled rows and cluttered blocks,
As we passed over them, what seemed a large estate
Extended
Below, green acres desolate,
Cleared, eerily,
Like a street for filming, a stone mansion fit
For English nobility,
Outhouses, water frontage. Stunned by it,
I lost it to the bridge, the Rocks,
Carried away. Before the flight had ended,
Though, coming down to earth like dark,
It suddenly struck me,
The psychiatric hospital, Callan Park,

Where I had worked, my first job out of school.
It all fell into place. But it hadn't looked like this.
What height
Gave out as stately spaciousness,
Held, then, below,
Proportions that were close yet ill-defined,
Like a filmshot that will show
A single vase and blur the room behind.
Each scheduled day was worked to rule
But existed out of time. And in white light
Each task, each movement through each hall,

Since no-one there could know
The whole, was clear but immaterial.

This is the occupational rule that trains
The range of vision down to details that subsume
Context,
Purpose, till, self-contained, they loom
As absolute
And meaningless. Details, conjured and dissolved
From job to job en route
Through a hidden network. That view, which evolved
Linkings of place and lives, remains,
On the ground, so many separate perplexed
Kafka heroes whom obsessions hound
In laughable pursuit
Of the inviolate castle's higher ground.

The world's too big. The map of our concerns,
Like ancient Greece, is marked out into petty jig-
Saw states
Based on the protocol of an egg,
Lilliput-style.
Inside, their matters feed the hours, hours feeding
On what life becomes while
Counting the e's in Anglo-Saxon, breeding
A green rose, or collecting urns;
Or stamping unread textbooks with due dates,
Dispensing onto evening trays
The coloured pills on file
That make these madmen sleep and dream their days.

Ghosts

1
Why is the table crowded? Only two
Are seated here. Why should their movements seem
Withheld, ungenerous, when the entire room
Is theirs and they're so intimate? The raw

Light's loud with memory though their talk is low.
Their speech is constant but their words can't claim
Its fluency; neither can they resume
Like children now the childhood tongue they know.

The sisters look, locked in familiar faces,
While shadows press between them, interpreters
Who subtly smudge the years and what they say.

With sweet distaste the exile of the cities
Stares while her sister, placing lips like kisses,
Slurps tea leaves from her cup and sucks them dry.

2
They are like the sunlight wasted on the wall
Of an abandoned building; like the stain
Beneath the eaves where rain had made a pool;
Furniture in the special room where no-one

Enters; the portrait someone might recall
That's wrapped and locked away, subject unknown:
Details of things, implicit, habitual,
About to matter or that mattered then.

How do they fill the space where we put life,
Whose time must be a stasis of regretting,
Or a green hope, bored for all the time we spend

Elsewhere? If they subsist in our belief,
Their end without it is this waiting, waiting
For an end. When it's already past the end.

3

In solitude the single bodies move.
In single choreography they pass
Through all their rooms, their dancing artifice
To draw from movement one whole life to live.

And while they grieve what they half like to grieve,
And miss someone they half prefer to miss,
The ghosts of their ideas, stroking them, bless
Fruitions they may offer but don't have.

Though lovers, like overlying images
That constitute one form, with separate lives
Perform the single body that each loves,

Alone, they chafe, each other's hostages;
Together, wide-eyed and with mouths aghast,
They claw for selves the other took and lost.

4

The witch in the grove, the spectre drawn from cold,
The walking cry along the woodland path,
The hybrid terror in the wastes of myth,
Take hold like an obsession and are held.

Lolling at noon, expectant, reconciled
To now, to this, the Sirens need no faith.
The sun draws the hot ocean up like breath
To wall them into purposes foretold

Them. This is forever then. Oars and sails
Give way to steam and to more subtle vessels,
But these pass by like shadows on the sun

Until the appointed one is willed, or wills.
Their time is always this time, and they've done
Nothing till now but this they now begin.

5

Two men stand by a single window, facing
It or, turning, pace the measure of the room;
But the pane reflects one only and each, pursing
To drink, tastes only his mouth on the rim.

Two women wait inside the same house, dressing,
Minding the same expanse of waiting time,
And comb their hair but feel no interlacing
Of strands electrified along the comb.

And when these women let these two men in
Two bodies take the place that should be four.
But the man she's kissing has no kiss for her,

And the man who gives it back she's never seen;
And the one he's stroking cannot feel his palm,
And the woman sighing is unknown to him.

Envoi

He's watched the silence lighten now for hours
Impassive blue. There is nothing there.
Whose place is this he does not occupy,
Though lying here? She is now downstairs.
Small clinks and soft talk float back up, and he
Is floating too between what he can't leave
And what he may not have.
He is nowhere.

The early silence, then, invades the house.
Do other households also wake out there,
Resisting this beginning? The baby lies,
Tagged to her favourite blanket like a price,
Hypnotized by sucking, though her eyes
Follow him past. Expressionless, unreached
By circumstance, detached,
She is nowhere.

In silence tea is drunk. A wordless touch
Fails to reclaim what never happened here.
The woman is relaxed, but not for him,
And smiles, though not for these events. They approach,
From different sides, departure. In the dim
Hall, self-absorbed, she stands and sways to her flute's
Cold interlude of notes,
And is nowhere.

Living

The cutlery goes here: here are the spoons,
Teaspoons in front, the larger ones behind.
The teatowel festoons
The righthand rail; to the left, since one's inclined
To symmetry, the handtowel is aligned.

This gold globe like an order holds the door,
Which might swing to in silence, open wide.
Ten. Morning tea. Before
My eyes a hand moves to the shelf to slide
The glass door back, and cup and saucer glide,

Balanced between four fingers and a thumb,
Towards the kettle's rushing. No other sound
But traffic's distant hum
Glides like a saucer on the silence. Drowned
In sun, the maidenhair's green fire, unbound,

Floats in a room I'm seldom drawn towards.
The heater's clock keeps all the hours by heart
Of night and day. It guards,
Red-eyed, the household's ritual, its art,
Whether I remain here or depart.

At night the fire chatters of itself.
The pages of my book take note and bend.
I watch a hand, a shelf,
A glass door slide. Saucer and cup attend
A rush like distant traffic without end.

Civilization

Sweeping gently down to the morning's blue,
The clipped green of the city gardens gives
That formal discourse for which they were grown,
The topos in which all this order lives,
Laid free within the limits of the view.

The walls, well-spaced and parallel in stone,
Might offer from the vantage of that height,
To hypothetical surveying eyes,
The unexpressed and decorous delight
Perspective grants. Below, river is shown,

And there, beyond, opposing roofs devise
Across a hill a subtle randomness.
The streets affect the way the hill inclines
Despite the rigour of their kerbed address.
This gives a tacit pleasure, like the wise

Plantings of native shrubs and tropic vines,
Encouraged to a nice untidiness
By scrupulous observance. Such looseness through
The marshalled suburbs presses like the hiss
Of an escape valve, holds their weight like lines

Of stress. So the slope supports the morning's blue
As paths direct these strolling democrats,
Their casual pomp among exotic trees
Whose lands of origin are mapless tracts
Which furnish here the limits of the view.

Disposed among these old formalities,
Our watcher sees this woman too, perhaps,
Changing her baby where she lets it lie,
Where, folding so and pinning so, she wraps
Its kicking form beneath the sibilant breeze,

Before the poised blue river and blue sky.

In a Dry Season

So each morning, which should be
Beginning, takes up the sense
Again. Wakers in that bleary lull
Are smiling, then, alert,
Feel their discontent return.
The clock seems harder and
The day heavy now in prospect.
These are the skies of tourist
Brochures. This warmth is like childhood,
The memory of summers,
But cannot convince. Something
Is not as it should be
And the lightscoured garden catches on
The eyes like grit, like wind.

Sitting indoors at tables they worry
The paper and do not
Take in the latest casualties,
Money's troubles. Chair legs
Creak from soles dragged on a dull
Linoleum. So one
Of them gets up to look outside.
But it's the same. Simply
To be now is to be displaced
And nothing is quite right.

Often of an afternoon they see
Their clouds, grown bruised and swollen,
Press on the city like a giant's
Foot. When they turn again
They've fled to the sky's far edge, white
And decorative. The light
Is so clear. Days bring no change.

Tenebrae

I

The entrance to Avernus is on Howrah Beach.
Oh yes, I've seen the ground subside
Beneath a she-oak where the sand
Funnelled into a chasm that might reach
Cathedral size somewhere below me, and
A grey sky slide
Downwards like a blanket from a bed.
Like flares above my head

The gulls performed their dying fall by wing and voice
With a perfect, heartless grace and sweep.
Old shelters, boatsheds had to tell
What always passes in them: LOVE ME BOYS,
SEX, XMAS 76. Why this is hell,
For we can't keep
What we are. Seaweed on wet rocks, its grip
Like clinging fingers, slipped.

II

So what is left? I listen to Roy Goodman sing
Allegri's *Mieserere,* a sound
Of disembodied beauty so pure
A Nero would have killed it, envying
A flawlessness he couldn't let endure.
But having found
A heartless perfection what else could he choose,
Lost in what he'd lose

When his voice broke? Like a light you've focused for too long
The last note clings. I hear the chant
Soothe and perturb the dark devout
When candle after candle is unsung
And a brief voice flares above them and goes out,
For at last they can't
Keep what they are and will endure the cost
Of being what is lost.

Building Space

So clear and common that you scarcely see
It there. The eyes glaze over what
Should bulk so large in paradox:
That spaced throughout the grid of the great city,
Set down like rocks
On a tarpaulin to keep it pinned
Against the empty wind,
The dull
Weight of churches embodies what is not,
Holding its ground in them, though they are null.

It's history's mighty effort to drag up
Stones in the name of nothing; words,
Idols, the will not to believe
That this is all there is, and it will stop,
However we've
Cried no, like children; fear of the known
That spends its faith in stone,
Trying
To purchase what no currency affords,
Confusing in the act the place of buying.

Inside, no doubt, cathedrals will put on
What they aspire to, when light,
As though it took their substance, falls,
Exposing them like film on which it's shone,
Dissolving walls
And columns. These visuals, however,
Merely serve to deliver
Them to
Their unreality. And here too, height
Framed and effaced by lighter measures, the true

Business of the city beside them climbs
With a quiet fervour, hides among
The sky in glassy walls whose return
Is curtained cloud and murals of sun, mimes
To blur or burn
The weight inside, made up of steel

And money, which is real.
And the door
That glides to your bidding leads where low-hung
Ceilings impend and air's too hard to draw.

So, like Magrittes that, being their own back-
Ground, disappear, they seem not there,
Though what goes on inside weighs out
Your days in their excesses and their lack,
While churches about
Them squat, solid as they seem
But being less, their scheme
Of grace
Largely contrived from nothing and despair,
An earthbound artifice of empty space.

Gauguin

Throughout their music you can hear this dream,
Vague scents, imagined islands, liquid suns,
A languor drained of any further wish.
Have they listened to these harmonies too long?

Vague scents, imagined islands, liquid suns,
Time and again their poets harp on this.
Have they listened to these harmonies too long?
A world of languid will, remote in heat,

Time and again their poets harp on this.
Perhaps his urging there was in their lines,
A world of languid will, remote in heat,
Where thought is a memory on the edge of sleep.

Perhaps his urging there was in their lines.
Back came his letters, lies of paradise
Where thought is a memory on the edge of sleep
Of something one might do, now so remote.

Back came his letters, lies of paradise,
Back came the fields of colour, desires drawn
Of something one might do, now so remote,
Vahines' sombre promissory eyes.

Back came the fields of colour, desires drawn
In eyes whose aspect was to picture his,
Vahines' sombre promissory eyes
From the Eden where his art had made them all.

The eyes whose aspect was to picture his
Perhaps at last reproached him to that move
From the Eden where his art had made them all
Pleasure-blind, to the place where they watched him;

Perhaps at last reproached him to that move,
Those faces where he'd wanted but one sense,
Pleasure-blind, to the place where they watched him,
Brilliant with anguish, wasted, asking, where?

Xanadu

When Marco floated
Once again alive
On memory's Venice
With his tales and millions
No-one credited,
Perhaps he too could believe
That he was lying, that his years
Of eastern service,
In the summer palace,
Under the cool pavilions,
Among intricate jade,
Had richly constructed
Like an art a sort of death,
Approaches to perfection through desires
Or dreams, the lies of faith.

For the Shang-tu
Marco walked in boast
Transferred his claim
To a place that no-one's
Visited, Xanadu —
The name shifting like a coast
To make unreal with change
The land, him
And his stories. And in time,
Enforced companions,
Hidden from who
They were by law
Of the city mute with myth,
All who live by language
Share Marco's death.

It's the trap of words
That leaves the fabulist entombed,
The stuff of dreams
That takes the dreamer
With it as the pageant fades,

Till Homer is assumed
To the side of Zeus, a learned
Litany of themes,
Some difficult names
And a foreign rumour;
Till Shakespeare avoids
Himself and bides
With his company of ghosts, to look
On speechless while his jokes are explained
And his verse goes blank.

Like copies taped
From copies the living speech
Is drowned at last
In a white noise.
Sea sighs trapped
In a shell that scarcely reach
The ear, the master voices
Singing from the past
On that changing coast
Awash with dictionaries
And scholia, report,
Word-perfect but
Ever more remote, the view
On the inexorable way that passes
From Shang-tu to Xanadu.

Destiny

It was a simple melody on two flutes,
Brief, meagre, somewhat plodding,
Unembellished,
A slight piece, as I thought, concluding
A side of *La Flûte Indienne.* What the notes
Said of it I forget, except its title,
Destino — Destiny. Destiny?
How did that name get itself attached
To a tune with so thin a
Resonance, that offered so little?

Yet, later, those narrow notes, that solemn fluting,
Playing on, played on the mind,
Thin and cold
As Andean air and its barren ground
That offers so little. And an image was competing,
Now recalled and Indian too, a hall
Of mummies, ancestors,
Trussed and rigid, upright underground, marshalled
There, bearing a bleak justice
That could prove perpetual,

Their dead mouths singing, singing, round and stretched,
Two opposite dry lines of O's,
Two hollow ranks
Of flutelike ceaseless crying that rose
Above hearing, and brought to mind the things you've wished
Never to know, what you hear
In lulls, behind all sounds,
Or when the first bird sings and its little chinks
Gather from the morning air
The whole weight of silence.